The Job of a CIVIC LEADER

Judge

Stephanie Gaston

Table of Contents

A Starfish Book

SEAHORSE PUBLISHING

Teaching Tips for Caregivers:

As a caregiver, you can help your child succeed in school by giving them a strong foundation in language and literacy skills and a desire to learn to read.

This book helps children grow by letting them practice reading skills.

Reading for pleasure and interest will help your child to develop reading skills and will give your child the opportunity to practice these skills in meaningful ways.

- Encourage your child to read on her own at home
- Encourage your child to practice reading aloud
- Encourage activities that require reading
- Establish a reading time
- Talk with your child
- Give your child writing materials

Teaching Tips for Teachers:

Research shows that one of the best ways for students to learn a new topic is to read about it.

Before Reading

- Read the "Words to Know" and discuss the meaning of each word.
- Read the back cover to see what the book is about.

During Reading

- When a student gets to a word that is unknown, ask them to look at the rest of the sentence to find clues to help with the meaning of the unknown word.
- Ask the student to write down any pages of the book that were confusing to them.

After Reading

- Discuss the main idea of the book.
- Ask students to give one detail that they learned in the book by showing a text dependent answer from the book.

Judge

A judge **presides** over a courtroom.

A judge makes sure that **trials** are fair.

To become a judge,
you must go to college.

You must understand laws.

Most judges were **lawyers** before they were judges.

Many judges work at local and state levels.

Some are elected by voters.

Some are chosen by officials in the city or state government.

Federal judges are chosen by the President of the United States.

Congress must approve the President's choices.

George W. Bush
43rd President
of the United States

John Roberts
Chief Justice
of the Supreme Court

Congress

Federal judges can work at District Courts or Courts of **Appeals**.

They can also serve on the highest court in the land, the Supreme Court.

Supreme Court of the United States

There are nine judges on the Supreme Court. They are called Supreme Court Justices. They keep their jobs for life.

Inside the courtroom,
judges wear black robes.

They sit on a platform
called a bench.

CHAMBERS
EXIT

It is the job of a judge to make sure each lawyer gets a chance to present their case.

One lawyer represents the person who says they have been harmed because a law was broken.

One lawyer represents the person who is **accused** of breaking the law.

After both sides argue their case, the judge makes a decision called a ruling.

If the judge decides that someone broke the law, they could go to jail.

Justice Thurgood Marshall was the first African American on the Supreme Court.

Justice Sandra Day O'Connor was the first woman on the Supreme Court.

Justice Thurgood Marshall
U.S. Supreme Court Justice
1967 to 1991

Justice Sandra Day O'Connor
U.S. Supreme Court Justice
1981 to 2006

A judge has an important job.

This leader upholds the laws of the United States.

WASHINGTON
OREGON
IDAHO
MONTANA
NORTH DAKOTA
MINNESOTA
WISCONSIN
MICHIGAN
NEW YORK
MAINE
MASSACHUSETTS
RHODE ISLAND
SOUTH DAKOTA
WYOMING
PENNSYLVANIA
NEW JERSEY
IOWA
NEBRASKA
NEVADA
ILLINOIS
INDIANA
OHIO
WEST VIRGINIA
VIRGINIA
UTAH
COLORADO
CALIFORNIA
KANSAS
MISSOURI
KENTUCKY
NORTH CAROLINA
TENNESSEE
ARIZONA
OKLAHOMA
NEW MEXICO
SOUTH CAROLINA
ARKANSAS
MISSISSIPPI
ALABAMA
GEORGIA
LOUISIANA
TEXAS
FLORIDA
ALASKA

Words to Know

accused (uh-KYOOZD): charged with breaking a law or having done something wrong

appeals (uh-PEELZ): second chances for people to have another trial and try to get a different ruling from a judge

Congress (KAHNG-gris): the lawmaking body of the United States made up of the Senate and the House of Representatives

federal (FED-ur-uhl): having to do with the government of an entire country instead of a city or state government; the national government of the United States

lawyers (LAW-yurz): people whose job is to represent people or governments in a court of law and to give advice about the law

presides (pri-ZIDES): rules over something; being in charge or having authority

trials (TRYE-uhlz): examinations of evidence in a courtroom to decide if a claim is true

Index

Comprehension Questions

1. It is a judge's job to make sure a trial is ____.
   a. short
   b. on the bench
   c. fair
2. The highest court in the United States is ____.
   a. the U.S. District Court
   b. the U.S. Supreme Court
   c. a Court of Appeal
3. **True or False:** Federal judges are chosen by the President of the United States.
4. **True or False:** Judges wear blue robes in the courtroom.
5. **True or False:** A judge must understand and follow the law.

Answers
1. c 2. b 3. True 4. False 5. True

About the Author

Stephanie Gaston is a journalist who has covered major stories including presidential inaugurations, natural disasters, and royal weddings. She has spent over a decade working in news for both local and major networks like CNN. Stephanie is a first-generation Haitian-American who grew up in Ft. Lauderdale, FL, a diverse community with Latin and Caribbean influences. In addition to being a writer, Stephanie is a dog lover, movie buff, fitness enthusiast, and most importantly, a proud mom.

Written by: Stephanie Gaston
Design by: Jen Bowers
Editor: Kim Thompson

Library of Congress PCN Data
Judge / Stephanie Gaston
The Job of a Civic Leader
ISBN 978-1-6389-7969-2 (hard cover)
ISBN 979-8-8873-5028-8 (paperback)
ISBN 979-8-8873-5087-5 (EPUB)
ISBN 979-8-8873-5146-9 (eBook)
Library of Congress Control Number: 2022941995

Printed in the United States of America.

Seahorse Publishing Company
www.seahorsepub.com

Published in the United States
Seahorse Publishing
PO Box 771325
Coral Springs, FL 33077

Photographs/Shutterstock: Cover and interior background circles © magic pictures, cover images ©2021 Gorodenkoff, ©2018 MIND AND I; p.3 legal pad ©2013 Mega Pixel, ©2013 sirtravelalot, ©2013 StudioSmart; p.4 ©2016 GOLFX; p.5 ©2021 Gorodenkoff; p.7 ©2019 Hunter Crenian, ©2016 AntonSokolov; p.9 Public Domain/Official portrait of U.S. Supreme Court/Steve Petteway, ©2012 Northfoto, ©2014 Drop of Light; p.11 Public Domain/Collection of the Supreme Court of the United States/Fred Schilling; p.12 ©2015 wavebreakmedia; p.13 ©2012 sirtravelalot; p.14 ©2017 r.classen; p.15 ©2022 Studio Romantic; p.17 ©2016 TaraPatta; p.19 Public Domain/National Archives and Records Administration/Yoichi Robert, ©2016 Rob Crandall; p.21 ©Fourleaflover, ©2022 Pickadook

SEAHORSE PUBLISHING